How Small Water Enterprises can contribute to the Millennium Development Goals

How Small Water Enterprises can contribute to the Millennium Development Goals

Evidence from Dar es Salaam, Nairobi, Khartoum and Accra

Gordon McGranahan, Cyrus Njiru,
Mike Albu, Mike Smith & Diana Mitlin

Water, Engineering and Development Centre
Loughborough University
2006

WEDC

Water, Engineering and Development Centre
Loughborough University
Leicestershire
LE11 3TU UK

A reference copy of this publication is also available online at:
http://wedc.lboro.ac.uk/publications/swe.htm

McGranahan, G., Njiru, C., Albu, M., Smith, M.D., and Mitlin, D. (2006)
*How Small Water Enterprises can contribute to the Millennium Development Goals:
Evidence from Dar es Salaam, Nairobi, Khartoum and Accra*

WEDC, Loughborough University, UK.

ISBN Paperback 1 84380 091 8

This document is an output from a project funded by the UK
Department for International Development (DFID)
for the benefit of low-income countries.
The views expressed are not necessarily those of DFID.

Designed and produced at WEDC by Kay Davey
Front cover photo montage by Rod Shaw
Front cover photographs by Cyrus Njiru

Printed by W & G Bairds onto Revive Silk: This material is recyclable and bio-degradable
and is a NAPM and Eugropa approved recycled grade

About the authors

Dr Gordon McGranahan, BA (Economics), MSc (Urban and Policy Sciences), PhD (Development/Economics). Dr Gordon McGranahan is a Development Economist with the International Institute for Development (IIED), and he currently directs the Human Settlements Group. Trained as an economist, he spent the 90s at the Stockholm Environment Institute, where he directed their Urban Environment Programme. He has published widely on environmental issues, with an emphasis on urban poverty and environmental problems in and around the home. Recent work on water includes co-authoring UN-Habitat's recent book on Water in the World's Cities: Local Action for Global Goals (Earthscan, 2003), co-authoring a review of private sector participation in water provision (Environment and Urbanization, 2003), and undertaking an analysis of how to ensure demand-side water management benefits low-income households. He has worked on tools for assessing water and sanitary conditions, including household surveys, participatory assessment and contingent valuation. His earlier work on water related issues is reflected in the urban report for the Comprehensive Assessment of the Freshwater Resources of the World (1997), which he co-authored.

Dr Cyrus Njiru, BSc (Civil Eng.), MSc, PhD, PGD San Eng, CEng, MICE, MCIWEM, FIEK, REng. Dr Cyrus Njiru is Research Manager at the Water, Engineering and Development Centre (WEDC), which is part of the Institute of Development Engineering at Loughborough University (UK). A Chartered Civil/Water and Sanitary Engineer, and also a Chartered Water and Environmental Manager, Cyrus has extensive water services and project management experience at senior level. He was previously Chief Manager of a national water company and holds degrees in Civil Engineering, Sanitary Engineering, Management and Implementation of Development Projects. His doctorate (PhD) degree was in the area of water services management, with a thesis on the integration of technical, financial, management and institutional aspects of water services.

Cyrus is currently involved in research in the general area of water supply and management, focusing on financial and institutional aspects of service delivery. He has published widely in professional and academic journals, and recently undertook research on pricing and service differentiation in the context of financing, cost recovery and demand management in low and middle income countries.

Mr Mike Albu, BSc, MSc. Enterprise Development Specialist, ITDG: Mike Albu is an engineer and policy researcher with 15 years experience in international development practice and management in African and south Asian countries. He currently works for Practical Action (the new name of ITDG), an international development agency working with poor communities to help them choose and use technology to improve their lives today and for generations to come. Mike specializes in design of interventions geared to making market systems work better in poor people's livelihoods – whether as entrepreneurs or as consumers of essential services. His current interests include participatory processes in value-chain analysis, developing markets for business services, and strategies for improving the business and institutional environment for micro-enterprise

Mr Mike Smith, MA, MSc. Mike Smith is Programme Manager at WEDC and also the WEDC MSc Programme Director. He is a Chartered Civil and Structural Engineer with wide experience of engineering aspects of development projects having a water focus. As well as teaching and training his interests are in the fields of water supply, wastewater treatment, sanitation, beneficial re-use of wastewater, and water quality. His overseas experience includes fieldwork and consultancy work in Lesotho, Sudan, Chad, Honduras, the Palestinian territories, India, China, Nepal and Peru. He has published several papers on a variety of water related issues, has supervised several PhD students, and co-authored the book "Out in the cold: emergency water supply and sanitation for cold regions" (WEDC, 1999) currently in its third edition.

Dr Diana Mitlin, BA (Econ), MSc (Econ), PhD. Social Development Specialist, IIED/IDPM. Diana Mitlin is a social development specialist who works primarily on issues related to urban poverty and civil society. In recent years, her activities have had a particular focus on the contribution made to development by the urban poor. Diana is a staff member at both the International Institute for Environment and Development and the Institute for Development and Policy Management (at the University of Manchester).

Acknowledgements

The financial support of the Department for International Development (DFID) of the British Government is gratefully acknowledged. The authors would also like to thank the following individuals and organizations for their valuable contribution to the research work, which provided the basis of this publication, especially members of the in-country research teams in Tanzania, Kenya, Sudan, and Ghana; and the review team members.

In-country research team in Tanzania:
Ms Vivienne Abbot, Mrs Wilhelmina Malima, Ms Mwanakombo Mkanga, Ms Sophia Komba and Mr. Mwita Maswa of WaterAid; and Mr Linus Materu of EWAREMA consultants; and Mrs Eda Gweba of Temeke Municipal Council

In-country research team in Kenya:
Isaack Oenga, David Kuria, Edward Marona, Janet Ngombalu, Ann Yoachim, Simon Okoth and Patrick Balla of ITDG Eastern Africa, Nairobi, Kenya.

In-country research team in Sudan:
Mohamed Elamin Abdel Gadir, Consultant (for ITDG Sudan).

In-country research team in Ghana:
Ms Aissa Toure, Stephen Ntow, Abdul Nasgiru and Emmanuel Addai of WaterAid Ghana; Mr Kwabena Sarpong Manu, Dr Kodjo Mensah-Abrampah and Paul Kukwaw of MIME Consult; and Mr George Acolor, E J Fosu, Nat Badoo, Mrs. Serena Kwakye-Minta, and W Amengor of Ghana Water Company.

Review team members:
Mr Jon Lane (Independent water and sanitation Consultant) and Dr Andrew Cotton of WEDC, Loughborough University, UK.

Contents

List of boxes

List of tables

Chapter 1

Summary

For centuries, Small Water Enterprises (SWEs) have supplied a large share of the water market in the urban centres of most low-income countries. Such SWEs have proved themselves economically viable, and often operate in competitive conditions. They extend water services to informal settlements that have little prospect of being supplied with piped water from the local utility. Unfortunately, they attract comparatively little investment, and even less support from governments. The incremental but critically important improvements they can provide tend to be overlooked by governments and international agencies. In international statistics any household that gets its water from vendors is defined as lacking access to improved water supplies (WHO and UNICEF 2000 - and see Box 2.2).

Greater private sector participation has been widely promoted in the water sector in recent decades (Finger and Allouche 2002). However, almost all of the attention has been devoted to large contracts open to international tender, and the handful of Northern-based multinationals that compete for them. This has, understandably, led to considerable controversy. Foreign dominated companies have been competing to be given the right to operate piped water networks; strategically important monopolies that used to be the responsibility of the public sector. In any case, large water companies typically have little experience of or inclination to operate in the poorest settlements (Budds and McGranahan 2003). Thus, the controversy has diverted attention from the places and enterprises most likely to improve water provision in low-income settlements.

This publication is based on a project designed to identify and test out ways of improving the water services delivered to the urban poor through SWEs (see Box 1.1 for a descriptive definition of SWEs). The project included fieldwork in a small number of African cities: Dar es Salaam (Tanzania); Nairobi (Kenya); Khartoum (Sudan) and Accra (Ghana). Even in these cities, where dependence on SWEs is undoubtedly high, the services provided by these SWEs are poorly documented.

SWEs have been found to conform far more closely to the free market ideal than do private utility operators. SWEs typically operate in highly competitive markets, and this competition keeps profits to a minimum, even in the absence of government regulation. Private utility operators, on the other hand, operate in highly regulated markets, partly to prevent monopoly pricing.

Yet government agencies have long been inclined to ignore or suppress SWEs. Little effort has been devoted to developing policies and actions that could improve the functioning of the SWEs, and hence the well-being of the households and individuals who depend upon them. This attitude is perhaps not as surprising as it seems. Even a well-functioning system of SWEs can be taken to reflect the failure of the government to supply piped water. And if SWEs go wrong, and sell contaminated or exorbitantly priced water, the government is likely to be blamed twice over. Partly because of such attitudes, however, important opportunities for improving water service delivery through SWEs are lost.

Box 1.1. What are Small Water Enterprises (SWEs)?

In many cities of Africa, Asia and South America, more than half the population of towns and cities obtain their water services from suppliers other than the official water supply utility. Numerous terms have been used to describe the various different types of unofficial service providers referred to in this report as Small Water Enterprises (SWEs). SWEs are private enterprises, usually operated by small-scale entrepreneurs (with a maximum of 50, and usually far fewer employees), which earn money from the sale of water.

SWEs typically provide water services alternative to, or supplementary to, those provided by water utilities. They usually supply water to places that are unserved or inadequately served by the utility, or at times when the utility cannot. Customers are not necessarily the poor: families from all income groups may rely on SWEs to provide all their water, or to provide additional supplies of water during periods of water rationing. In many cities, however, it is low-income households that are worst served by the utility and most dependent on SWEs.

SWEs may obtain their water from natural sources (e.g. wells) or from the piped water network (either formally or illicitly). Three broad categories of SWEs are:

- Wholesale vendors (e.g. tanker operators), who obtain water from a source and sell the water on to consumers and distributing vendors;

- Distributing vendors who obtain water from a source or from a wholesale vendor, and sell the water directly to consumers, via door-to-door sales (including in some cases small piped networks); and

- Direct vendors, who sell water direct to consumers who come to collect and pay for water at the source. This category includes household resellers and operators of water kiosks.

In each of the cities considered in this report, local teams have worked to identify constraints, opportunities and strategies for enabling small water-providing enterprises to deliver acceptable water services to low-income urban consumers. The next stage of the project will involve testing a selection of the improvements identified in two of the cities. The accumulated evidence suggests that there are numerous opportunities for enhancing the role of SWEs in all of the cities. To seize these opportunities, however, will require significant changes in relations between SWEs, water utilities and in some cases other actors – standard operating procedures often serve to reproduce existing constraints on SWEs.

A common obstacle to improving SWEs, whether they involve operating kiosks in Dar es Salaam or Nairobi, donkey carts in Khartoum, tankers in Accra, or one of the many other types of SWEs found in these four cities, is that they have not traditionally been considered to be legitimate suppliers. The goal of the utility has been assumed to be one of replacing rather than assisting the SWEs. The government responsibility with regard to SWEs has been to prohibit them from selling 'overpriced' or 'substandard' water, rather than in encouraging them to invest or compete more vigorously.

Perhaps this is why, in all of the cities, the interface between the utility and the SWE water systems was found to be a major source of problems. The SWE water systems meet important basic needs, but do not function as well as they should. In some places, regulations suppress supplies without any discernable impact on the quality of provision. The cart operators in Khartoum, for example, view the public health regulations as just another excuse used by local officials use for harassing them, rather than a reason for taking greater care in water delivery. Often, the illegitimate character of SWEs has inhibited the investments that would improve the reliability or quality of supplies. This lack of investment applies to both the utilities, who fail to invest in servicing the SWEs, and to the SWEs themselves, who cannot secure finance at competitive rates.

In all of these cities, however, the situation is changing, and there are new opportunities for developing more vigorous and economically efficient SWE systems. Sectoral reforms are providing more opportunities for small, as well as large, private enterprises. Governments are more inclined to recognise the strengths of the SWEs. Utilities are being encouraged to work with, rather than against, SWEs. There remains a great deal to be learned about how governments, utilities and SWEs can work more effectively together, but the desire to learn is evident, and with good reason.

Provided these lessons can be learned, one can expect a number of benefits, particularly for low-income neighbourhoods:
- Greater customer convenience, as SWEs become more reliable and accountable.
- Lower prices, as supplies from SWEs increase.
- Less of a burden from water-related diseases, as hygiene improves.

The utility can also expect to benefit from:
- less water lost, as SWEs invest in better equipment (and numbers of illegal connections fall); and
- higher utility revenues, as SWEs become legitimate and reliable paying customers.

Improvements in the services delivered by SWEs are still likely to fall short of the ideal of piped water in every home. However, as described below, for hundreds of millions of urban dwellers a narrow focus on extending piped water provision is counterproductive. Improvements in SWEs, on the other hand, can not only make a critical difference, but can represent progress towards the long term ideal.

Chapter 2

The importance of SWEs for the urban poor

The aim of the project upon which this synthesis report is based is to find means to improve water services for the urban poor, and thereby to improve their well-being. The focus is on SWEs operating in informal urban settlements that have developed largely outside the formal planning system, often on contested land. Before considering how water provisioning by SWEs can be improved, it is worth considering how important they already are, and why they are likely to remain important for the foreseeable future, especially for the urban poor.

In low-income towns and cities, a large share of small enterprises and residences are informal; they are unrecognised, unregistered or do not conform to the formal planning regulations. As illustrated by the city studies of Dar es Salaam, Nairobi, Khartoum and Accra summarized below, large numbers of citizens are not connected to the formal piped water network. This is not exceptional but simply reflects the level of informal settlement in these cities. Informality has been and will continue to be widespread, not only in Africa but in many parts of the world. In 1991, a study of nine Asian countries concluded that between 40 and 95 per cent of all households had no possibility of living in a dwelling produced by the formal sector (ESCAP 1991). Secure tenure, housing and services are acquired incrementally (progressively) because they are otherwise unaffordable. Statistics on cement production and use indicate that 70 per cent of housing investment in Mexico is probably occurring incrementally (Ferguson 2004). In Tanzania it is estimated that 98 per cent of the housing stock in urban areas is constructed on an incremental basis (Mutagwaba quoted in Government of Tanzania and UN-Habitat 2003). This is unchanged from the figures quoted for 1978 (Okpala 1994). In the Philippines a similar estimate is that 93 per cent of owner occupied houses have been built through an incremental building process (Ballesteros 2002). Such figures illustrate the significance of incremental development. Land is acquired informally (although not necessarily illegally) and upgrading is also informal and rarely conforms to planning regulations.

The notion that the only important improvements in water provision come through the expansion of piped water supplies is dangerously misleading. Numerous factors prevent the formal piped water networks from reaching households in informal settlements. At the level of the formal provider, there are problems with the scale of capital investment, the regulatory capacity and in some cases with the legality of the settlement. At the household level, there may be difficulties in obtaining sufficient funds for connections and associated costs, and sufficient tenure security to give people the incentive to invest in pipes and connections. Even if the lower prices charged for piped water in comparison to privately vended water appear to make the costs affordable, there may be significant difficulties in raising the funds required for capital costs (and in making the regular monthly payments that are generally required). Some lending programmes have been established, but many micro-finance agencies require some degree of legal tenure before they offer loans. In other cases even a formal land title is not sufficient to secure a loan, and evidence of formal employment may be required. Complicating matters further, low-income households are often forced to settle on precarious sites, that are also difficult to reach with piped water networks.

In short, large numbers of urban households in low-income countries will not be reached with piped supplies in the foreseeable future. It is important to work to remove the financial, institutional and technical obstacles to extending piped water supplies; but it is equally important to improve water provision for households that will not be connected to the piped water system. In the absence of piped water supplies, informal water vendors are often a central part of the local reality, and play an important role. In an urban context in which households have to manage within labour and commodity markets, some households are willing to reduce their collection times and purchase supplies from small entrepreneurs who, in most cases, collect from the piped network at some distance from the settlement. Where there is deterioration in the piped network, this may also encourage some households living in more formal neighbourhoods to buy water from water vendors. In the long run, the ideal may be piped water connections for everyone; but the pursuit of this ideal must not be allowed to undermine the incremental improvements that, for the foreseeable future, will remain a more realistic aspiration for hundreds of millions of urban dwellers.

Section 2.1 below gives a brief review of the role of SWEs in urban Africa, Asia and Latin America. SWEs are not well documented, and display great diversity. This diversity would seem to reflect an ability to adapt to local and changing circumstances. Anecdotal claims that SWEs exploit the urban poor and make large profits have not been substantiated, and probably reflect extreme circumstances. Indeed, reviews undertaken in recent years indicate that while the services SWEs provide are rarely of the quality of a piped connection to the network of a well run water utility, in the right circumstances they can provide adequate services at reasonable prices. More generally, there is a great deal of evidence of SWEs playing an important positive role where utility networks are absent or not functioning well.

Sections 2.2 to 2.5 review the role of SWEs in Dar es Salaam, Nairobi, Khartoum and Accra, with an emphasis on their operation in selected informal settlements. Again, there is considerable diversity, both between and within cities, in the types of SWEs and chains of supply through which residents of informal settlements obtain their water. Yet from the water yards and donkey carts of Khartoum to the borehole operators and itinerant vendors of Dar es Salaam, SWEs play an important role in all of the cities, and particularly in informal settlements. Moreover, while many of these SWEs could be described as informal enterprises, they are almost all heavily influenced by government policies and utility practices.

Finally, section 2.6 examines how the operations of the SWEs in these informal settlements impact on the urban poor. Even within informal settlements, residents face different levels and forms of poverty, and a convenient and affordable service for one resident may be insufficiently reliable for another, and beyond the reach of yet another. For some residents SWEs provide employment, and here yet another set of issues and opportunities come into play.

2.1 An overview of SWEs in urban centres of Africa, Asia and Latin America

The role of SWEs in urban water supply

Several surveys have shown that SWEs serve a significant percentage of urban residents in Africa, Asia and South America (Conan 2003). In many cities, SWEs account for a greater share of the water market than the official utilities. SWEs are able to complement the services provided by water utilities, and to extend water coverage into areas that have little prospect of being served by utility supplies.

SWEs typically provide services in areas where water supplies are intermittent, or where there is inadequate network supply. Examples of situations where SWEs have overcome difficulties encountered by utilities include high-level areas to which water utilities will not deliver water, areas subject to flooding, illegal settlements, and where low water consumption makes utility supplies uneconomical. Even in some areas of cities that are served by utilities, SWEs are able to compete with the utilities in provision of water services for the poor and the not-so-poor. Globally it is widely acknowledged that the pace of urbanisation is outstripping the ability of many water utilities to provide services for new customers, or even to maintain service standards for existing customers. In Africa, Asia and South America, SWEs are therefore likely to remain as one of the few realistic options for water delivery in some parts of towns and cities for the foreseeable future.

In many places where the utility is facing difficulties expanding, for example recently in Guatemala City and Lima, SWE activities expand more rapidly than the formal piped water network (Solo 1998). A World Bank-supported project is assisting the local utility in Lima to expand its services, but the rapid expansion of SWE activities in Lima is without the benefit of long-term financial assistance. Many utilities experience difficulty both in keeping pace with population increases and in adequately maintaining existing facilities. In some places, SWEs extend the piped network into unserved areas. In others, they provide a substitute supply in areas where the utility supply is deteriorating.

SWE activities are a source of local employment, often providing more jobs within the water sector than the local water utility (Kjellén and McGranahan 2004). Water carriers, who transport relatively small quantities of water, are generally the largest group of SWEs. Those who sell water from stationary sources (e.g. kiosks) or from tankers can supply large quantities of water without employing many workers (Kjellén and McGranahan 2004).

The roles of SWEs in supplying water are summarised in Table 2.1.

Table 2.1. Characteristics of SWEs in the water supply sector	
Typical market speciality	Filling gaps in service supply
	Filling niche markets
	Serving markets with low entry and investment costs
Relative competencies	SWEs have good local knowledge
	SWEs are innovative in their use of local resources
	SWEs are responsive to the demands of the poor
	SWEs can operate in competitive markets
Potential disadvantages	Quality controls are difficult to implement and enforce for informal enterprises
	There is limited scope for investment
	SWEs have difficulty in achieving substantial economies of scale
Potential advantages for the urban poor	Responsiveness: SWEs can provide services where other service providers will not or cannot go
	SWEs will sell small volumes of water and accept small individual payments for water supply
	SWEs may be willing to offer credit or agree to convenient payment schemes
	Flexibility: SWEs are adaptable and can tailor their services to the specific physical and social characteristics of the neighbourhood

Source: Adapted from McGranahan and Owen (2004)

The variety of SWE activities

In every country where they operate, SWEs respond to local conditions and find ways to fill niche markets for water. There is, therefore, considerable variety in the nature and scale of SWE activity, depending upon local circumstances such as water resources, topography, utility service levels, and the regulatory framework. Various different types of SWEs usually operate in parallel within the same city or settlement, serving different categories of customer (Kjellén and McGranahan 2004). Some SWEs work independently, while some hire equipment such as carts, or are employed by others who take a percentage of the income from water sales. Five types of SWE are described briefly below.

1. **Resales** – Individual households that have piped water supplies often sell water on to neighbours, either in small quantities, or through extensions to the piped network. Residential resales often supplement other water services, such as

public standposts and water kiosks, that are unable to meet the needs of the local population. Households that sell water can recover their regular costs, while offering informal purchase arrangements and credit to their customers. In Bamako (Mali) 25% of water supplies are through resales (Solo 1998). Even in areas where resale of water is illegal, utilities often privately acknowledge that SWE activities are a consequence of the utility's inability to supply water adequately to all customers. Utility staff are therefore often reluctant to take action against those who sell water, and may modify their practices to accommodate SWE activities. In Accra, for example, where resale of water is illegal, SWEs pay commercial water tariffs, indicating that the utility has modified its practice in the knowledge that resale occurs. In several cities, SWEs have concessions to sell water from kiosks. Kiosk operators are in a strong position, but they need to rely on local goodwill, so need to keep their prices down.

2. **Distributing SWEs – water carriers** – Water carriers operate widely in many cities in Africa, Asia and South America. For a variety of reasons many urban households find it preferable to purchase water from water carriers than to fetch their own water. Carrying water is a physically demanding activity, and water carriers may use plastic or metal containers either carried manually or on hand-carts, bicycles or animal-drawn carts. Water carriers are usually males from low-income households similar to the households they serve.

3. **Distributing SWEs – tankers** – Tanker lorries are able to deliver large volumes of water, but the capital required to purchase and maintain a tanker is a major obstacle to entry into this SWE market. Tankers are less common than water carriers, often serving higher-income customers and customers who require bulk supplies of water.

4. **Private water supplies** – In some locations, alternative water sources may be used in addition to utility water supplies. SWEs may obtain water from groundwater sources (via wells). In several places supplies from SWEs using groundwater sources exceed 30% of the total local supply. Solo (1998) cites, as examples, Tegucigalpa (Honduras), Lima (Peru), Guatemala City, and parts of Turkmenistan and Uzbekistan.

5. **Bottled or pre-packed water** – Sales of small volumes of bottles or sealed containers of water reflect a relatively recent business development. This is probably in response to increased income levels, higher aspirations, and

the perceived poor quality of water supplied by some utilities. The scale of businesses ranges from small enterprises that produce sealed plastic bags filled with water, to large businesses producing bottled spring or mineral waters. Various authors (for example: Conan 2003; Khan and Siddique 2000) give examples of such enterprises. Instances of SWEs selling water in sachets were also encountered in Accra during the current study.

For some SWE activities, such as for water carriers, entry into the water vending market may be easy, requiring little or no investment. If entry is easy, however, the market is usually competitive, and these SWEs have no guaranteed customers. They therefore need to attract and retain enough loyal customers to remain in business. Customers may receive regular supplies of water from a specific SWE, or may receive some or all of their supplies from any of the SWEs operating locally.

Although unpaid work associated with collection and management of water in households is generally the responsibility of women, men tend to dominate the paid SWE work sector. There are a few exceptions to the difference in gender roles: female kiosk attendants are fairly common (and are perceived to be less corrupt than male counterparts), and in Dakar some women work as SWEs, carrying water containers on their heads (Kjellén and McGranahan 2004).

Regulation

In considering how to regulate SWEs, a key message of this report is that the indirect costs of regulation (e.g. reduced water supplies) must be set against the gains (e.g. a low risk of water contamination). Despite all their local diversity, one of the most common afflictions of SWE regulation is that standards are set so high that SWEs cannot comply without drastically reducing water provision. In many circumstances the very activity of selling water privately is officially prohibited. Such regulations are rarely enforced rigorously – local officials are likely to be all too aware that enforcing such regulations strictly would do more harm than good. But intermittently enforced regulations can easily provide opportunities for corruption, and undermine the regulatory process. Under most circumstances, effective regulation is regulation that supports incremental improvements in SWE provisioning, and does not impose a burden on those SWEs that are providing vital services.

Regulation of SWEs is made more difficult by the number and variety of SWEs and of the markets they serve. Overly bureaucratic registration and inspection systems are sometimes ignored, and at other times abused. In Tanzania water carriers are supposed to carry small business licences, but this requirement is widely ignored by both the SWEs and the authorities (Kjellén and McGranahan 2004). Alternatively, SWEs using donkey carts in Khartoum face regular harassment from officials who are apparently more interested in extracting money than in improving standards.

Formal or informal agreements have been reached among SWEs in some cities, and can provide the basis for indirect regulation. Tanker drivers in Accra have formed an association, but most SWEs operate on the basis of informal agreements. Agreements may break down as circumstances change, such as during water shortages, when some individual SWEs will operate in their own interests, charging higher prices and operating outside their usual territory (Kjellén and McGranahan 2004). Perhaps more important, agreements among SWEs will not always serve the interests of customers, and may inhibit healthy competition. Cairncross and Kinnear (1991) describe a project in Khartoum aimed at assisting in income generation for people from Southern Sudan. Northern Sudanese controlled the water source, so Southerners were prevented from using it. The existence of the cartel only became apparent when it was challenged.

In short, it is important not to assume that regulation needs to involve formal rules prescribing how SWEs should operate. Voluntary regulation, responding to complaints, and facilitating negotiated settlements are also important forms of regulation. Even these forms of regulation need to be used with care, however.

2.2 SWEs in Dar es Salaam

Most of the urban poor in Dar es Salaam live in informal settlements, where the utility has not extended its water networks. Water services in these informal urban settlements are provided predominantly by SWEs. Most of these settlements face serious water supply problems, but without the SWEs the problems would be far worse. Moreover, along with the many other informal enterprises that populate these settlements, SWEs provide much needed employment and income earning opportunities.

The importance of SWEs in providing water services in Dar es Salaam is illustrated in Table 2.2., which contains estimates of Utility and SWEs' service coverage. These estimates had to be derived from a combination of utility information and household survey results because, despite their evident importance, SWEs are often neglected in surveys of household water use. Overall, the various vendors are estimated to supply more than half of the population.

Box 2.1. Study design:
The selection of informal settlements and respondents in Dar es Salaam, Nairobi, Khartoum and Accra

To understand the contribution of SWEs to addressing the water needs of the urban poor, the study examined informal settlements within each of the cities of Dar es Salaam, Nairobi, Khartoum and Accra. The same selection criteria was used in each city. Informal settlements and interviewees within the settlements were chosen as follows:

Tanzania: In Dar es Salaam, *Sandali* was selected from among the 54 major informal urban settlements identified by the Sustainable Dar es Salaam Project. On the basis of information from the Sustainable Dar es Salaam Project, and the study team's criteria, both Yombo Vituka and Sandali were identified as suitable locations. Sandali ward was given priority because it has a sub ward that receives very intermittent utility supplies, and is served by a wide variety of SWEs. Interviews and focus group discussions were held with both households and small water enterprises. Altogether in depth interviews were conducted with 20 households, and there were 5 focus group discussions with local residents. Among the small enterprises, there were 12 in depth interviews and four focus group discussions.

Kenya: *Maili Saba,* an informal settlement situated about 10 kilometres east of Nairobi city centre, was selected. Maili Saba was ranked 4th when selecting study areas in Nairobi under a scoring system that included eight criteria: high density, no piped supplies, illegal land tenure, poor supply volume, no inspection of water, poor access to water, direct vending and the land being owned by neither the city council nor private developers. However, Maili Saba was easier to access, since the research institution had some ongoing activities in the area. Moreover, Maili Saba was favoured because it is more directly influenced by developments in Nairobi than the top ranked settlements. A total of 34 enterprises and 66 consumers were randomly selected for interviewing.

Sudan: *Soba Al Aradi* (on the southern periphery of Al Khartoum) and *Dar Al Salam* (on the western periphery of Umm Durman) were selected in Khartoum as they have planning department recognition, are not liable to demolition, feature high poverty levels, poor services and are very unlikely to be connected to piped water in the near future. Both locations rely on water yards for supplies and the majority of households are served by donkey cart vendors (the most common itinerant water vendors in Khartoum). Households were selected for interviewing on the basis of the customer lists of ten randomly selected donkey cart vendors in each of the locations. The lists were stratified into three according to proximity to the water yard, and one household from each stratum was chosen for interview, yielding a total of 30 households.

Ghana: A number of factors were considered in selecting the sites of *Teshie and Ashalley Botwe* in Accra, including legality of settlement, current water service, age and morphology of the community, and finally economic and social characteristics. Both are central but informal settlements with low-income levels that are not adequately served with water, but Teshie is an indigenous settlement while Ashalley Botwe is a mixed group settlement. Most of Teshie is off the piped water network, and where the piped network is present water has not been flowing for the past three years. The utility claims the pipes are very old and need to be changed, while the residents allege that their supplies are being cut off in favour of high-income areas in adjoining communities. Fourteen households were surveyed in each area, along with a total of 20 tanker operators and 20 vendors.

Table 2.2. Percentage coverage by various water service providers in Dar es Salaam	
Type of water supplier	**Estimated coverage (percentage of population)**
Utility water coverage through direct connections	42%
Communal utility kiosks	4%
Utility water resellers	35%
Tanker trucks	2%
Pushcart vendors	2%
Private and communal boreholes	13%
Unprotected sources	2%
Total	**100%**

Types of SWEs and how they operate

The types of SWEs operating in Dar es Salaam comprise the following:

- street water vendors using pushcarts to transport water in jerry cans to consumers and to small business enterprises;
- private water boreholes and kiosks supplying water to consumers and water vendors at the supply point sources or through distribution network;
- communal water boreholes and kiosks supplying water to consumers and water vendors at the supply point sources;
- household resellers of utility water to neighbours; and
- wholesale transporters of water using tanker trucks to supply water to mostly wealthier customers in far away settlements.

Most SWEs, with the exception of wholesale transporters, deliver water supply services in the low- income informal settlements.

SWEs in Dar es Salaam are owned and run by either single individuals (e.g. most pushcart and tanker truck operators), family members (most private boreholes and resellers of utility water), or community water committees (most community managed boreholes and kiosks). Some SWEs are quite formalised.

Assessment of supply chains in Dar es Salaam

Supply chains relate to all activities involved in the flow of water from service providers with bulk supply or source, through different means of transportation to the end-user. The major actors in the supply chain include water suppliers, water distributors and water customers. Water is supplied through direct transportation from the source by consumers themselves, through private piped systems or through street water vendors who transport the water in jerrycans loaded on push carts. Payment flows in the opposite direction. The principal supply chains in the settlement studied in Dar es Salaam are illustrated in Table 2.3.

Table 2.3. Supply chains in Dar es Salaam	
Supply Chain	**Customer**
Surface water→City water→Communal kiosk→Consumer	~3% of households
Surface water→City water→Communal kiosk→Pushcart Vendor→Consumer	~1% of households
Surface water→City water→Utility water reseller→Consumer	~15% of households Used in both medium and low-income areas where few households have connections
Surface water→City water→Utility water reseller→Pushcart vendor→Consumer	~1% of households
Aquifer→Private borehole→Tanker truck→Consumer	~1% of households Used in high and middle-income areas where there is good road access
Surface water→City water→City water kiosk→Tanker truck→Consumer	~1% of households Used in high and middle-income areas where there is good road access
Aquifer→Communal and private boreholes→Consumer	~60% of households Important from considerations of volumes and affordability
Aquifer→Private borehole→Pushcart Vendor→Consumer	~20% of households Important in terms of volume and reliability.

Water suppliers include utilities (DAWASA, City Water Services and Municipalities), private borehole owners, community managed boreholes and kiosks, and resellers of utility water.

Water distributors include:
- Street water vendors who transport water usually in six 20-litre jerrycans using pushcarts. Street water vendors are both retailers and wholesalers of water. Payment is mostly made on delivery, or on a monthly basis for a few reliable consumers with stable incomes.

- Water tanker operators (capacity 7,000 – 10,000 litres) who transport water using trucks. The water is usually sold wholesale to wealthier households located away from informal settlements. Water is also delivered wholesale to construction sites by tanker trucks. Payment is made either every time water is delivered to a customer or on a monthly basis.

Customers of SWEs' services include the following:
- poor households;
- small business enterprises using water (local brewers, local food vendors, restaurants, guest houses) in the informal settlements; and
- wealthier families living in high-income areas without adequate supply (who generally purchase water from tanker trucks).

Water supplied by the utility (City Water Services) directly to communal kiosks offers the cheapest supply chain option. Other chains of supply are of higher cost to the consumer due to associated costs for transporting water. Although the communal kiosk supply chain option provides water of good quality, the reliability of supply is constrained by the utility rationing pattern and the lack of water storage tanks at the kiosks. There is competition from connected resellers of utility water who have installed storage tanks.

2.3   SWEs in Nairobi
Nairobi, even more so than Dar es Salaam, lacks significant local surface or ground water sources. Well over 90% of the population depends on distant water sources managed by the Nairobi City Water and Sewerage Company (NCWSCL) – principally the Ng'ethu Reservoir, as well as Ruiru and Sasumua Dams.

Less than half the urban population, however, has a legitimate household connection to NCWSCL's piped network. Well over a million people obtain NCWSCL water through other means, principally through SWEs. For the most part these water consumers are poor people inhabiting the informal urban settlements, often near the municipal boundaries, which are not covered by NCWSCL's distribution network.

In a typical settlement, such as Maili Saba where this research was conducted, the principal role of SWEs is to deliver NCWSCL's bulk water from the utilities mains pipelines – some 2 or 3 kms away – into the settlement where it can be retailed.

In addition, SWEs fulfil other important functions:
- They protect against short-term supply intermittency by providing (limited) tank storage capacity.
- They protect against seasonal supply shortages by investing in alternative water sources (principally groundwater extraction through boreholes).
- They provide door-step delivery services for households and small businesses unable or unwilling to carry water from retail points.

Types of SWES and how they operate
The functions above dictate the forms that the Nairobi SWEs typically take, i.e:

- **Private kiosks** (owner managed) – with ad-hoc, usually substandard, piped connections to the NCWSCL mains.
- **Manual vendors** – usually using bicycles or hand-carrying jerry-cans of water from kiosks, boreholes or other unprotected sources to homes and local small businesses.
- **Private boreholes** (owner managed) – extracting groundwater (often of dubious quality).

Supply chains
During most of the year, the most important supply chains involving SWEs are those illustrated in Table 2.4. These two routes account for about 90% of water consumed in Maili Saba, since alternatives are limited. Poorer households use river water for laundry and washing. However, seasonal factors are important, since NCWSCL supply can be unreliable during protracted dry spells. At these times residents may rely more on boreholes, unprotected wells or even the local river for cooking and drinking water.

At the time of the research, kiosks in Maili Saba served some 3300 households. Each household consumes an average of 0.16 m^3/day (i.e. 60 m^3/yr) and is on average about 250 metres from the nearest kiosk.

Table 2.4. Supply chains in Maili Saba	
Supply chain	**Customer**
NCWSCL→Private Kiosk→Consumer	84% households
NCWSCL→Private Kiosk→Manual Vendor→ Consumer	16% households, small businesses and construction sites

Private kiosk owners typically pay for a legitimate or semi-legitimate connection with the NCWSCL pipeline, and then invest in a low-cost pipeline to transfer water to their own kiosk. These pipelines – being plastic and shallow buried – are prone to deliberate or accidental damage, and frequently leak. Some kiosk owners have modest storage tanks to mitigate against intermittent breakdown in supplies.

The costs of establishing kiosks and their piped connections, including bribes and dues paid to utility officials, local slum-lords and politicians, can be high (US$300 – 1000). Maintaining the connections can also be expensive. These costs are recovered through hefty mark-ups. Bulk water purchased by kiosk owners from NCWSCL for US$0.20 /m³, normally sells for US$2.50 /m³. This rises to as much as US$5.00 /m³ during times of shortage.

Whether this represents a good return on the kiosk investment is unclear, since the cost of bribes and other rents is difficult to ascertain with accuracy. Clearly though, the actual NCWSCL water tariff itself represents only a very small part of the SWE's total costs.

There does not appear to be much competition between kiosks, and nor is there rapid entry of new players into the kiosk owning market. Presumably this is because the process of setting up in business, particularly getting connected and licensed, is cumbersome and lacking transparency.

Manual vendors tend to be either bicycle users (predominantly male), or back-loaders (predominantly female). They provide a portage service using 20 litre jerry cans, serving better off households, small businesses and the needs of construction sites. The effective charge for this service (US$6 - 18 /m³) seems to depend on the distance carried.

Manual vendors have low status in the community, their business activity is not licensed and consequently they suffer frequent harassment by various officials and local slum-lords. It seems that a significant percentage of their income may be being diverted by this means.

2.4   SWEs in Khartoum

The three cities of Greater Khartoum, including Al Khartoum, Al Khartoum Bahri and Umm Durman (Omdurman) rely on both surface water from the river Nile, and ground water from deep and shallow aquifers beneath the cities.

Nile water extraction, treatment and distribution is managed by Khartoum State Water Corporation (KSWC) through their increasingly ancient infrastructure. This network serves 210,000 household connections in the centre of the city. However, very rapid urban expansion in the past two decades has left around four million people now living in very extensive informal settlements and former displaced people's camps outside the reach of KSWC's distribution network.

The people who inhabit these peri-urban informal settlements are predominantly rural migrants who have fled drought, civil war and destitution in Sudan's regions. They are not only extremely poor, but also marginalised by religious and ethnic differences. Overwhelmingly, these people rely on groundwater extracted through deep boreholes at around 900 official extraction points, known as 'water yards', around the city. The quality of water extracted here is generally high, but many of the water yards are dilapidated or in disrepair.

Like the Nile surface water infrastructure, water yards are the responsibility of KSWC, even though most were initially installed by NGOs. Now that many are badly neglected, KSWC is looking for better ways to manage and maintain them, including through private management (ie. SWEs).

In typical settlements, such as Soba Al Aradi and Dar Al Salam where this research was conducted, the principal role played by SWEs however is merely to deliver water from the KSWC water yard to household door-steps where it is retailed.

In addition, SWEs in Khartoum fulfil other important functions:
- They provide households with access to more distant water yards when the local one is out of order.
- They sometimes provide flexible payment arrangements tailored to their customers needs.
- They deliver water from low-quality sources such as old irrigation ditches and wells to construction sites.
- They are starting to become involved in management of water yards under contract from KSWC.

Types of SWES and how they operate

The functions above dictate the forms that the Khartoum SWEs typically take, that is:

- **Mobile cart operators** – with donkey-drawn water carts that shuttle between water yards, homes and construction sites.
- **Licensed water yard management agents** – who are just starting to emerge as players, alongside community-managed water yard committees.

Assessment of supply chains in Khartoum

The principal supply chains in the informal settlements studies in Khartoum are those illustrated in Table 2.5.

Table 2.5. Supply chains in Dar Al Salam and Soba al Aradi	
Supply chain	**Customer**
KSWC Water yard→Cart Operator→Consumer	80% of households in peri-urban settlements, construction sites and small businesses
KSWC Water yard→Consumer	Low income households within short walking distance of functioning water yards
Shallow Wells→Cart Operator→Consumer	Construction sites, poorest households not close to water yards

Each operational water yard typically serves 600 – 1000 households, and may be served by 30 to 50 cart operators – each making seven to ten round trips a day with a 380 litre tank. For the cart operator, delivery distances range from 50 - 750 metres, increasing to 2 kilometres when the nearest water yard is out of order.

At the time of the study, KSWC had only licensed around 20 private water yard management agents on an experimental basis. These SWEs are required to provide financial collateral and show technical competency. Prices at the water yard are fixed by the utility (US$ 0.80 /m^3) and revenue is shared. The long-term viability of these businesses is still uncertain since aside from fuel for pumping, the main costs of water yard operation are unpredictable: repair and replacement of equipment. Most of the community-managed water yards have run into difficulties in this regard.

Cart operators are typically young men with few assets, often using hired animals and carts. The work is of low status and extremely arduous, and there are few entry barriers to the business. Competition for both customers and access to water is often intense, with long delays common at water yards.

Water yard charges only make up about 28% of the doorstep price of water (typically US$3.00 /m^3). Animal fodder and cart hire costs US$1.30 /m^3 on average. Licence fees, bribes and duties paid to officials also take at least US$0.15 /m^3 from the cart operators' income, as well as costing time and inconvenience.

2.5   SWEs in Accra

In spite of efforts to increase access to potable water supply in Ghana, the gap between demand and supply has continued to widen. Both rich and poor are affected. Ghana Water Company (GWC) reports an average water coverage of 59% of residents in the urban areas – an estimate which is likely to be optimistic. The gap left to be filled by SWEs and private sources is therefore at least 41%. Most of the unserved are estimated to be the poor living in areas without a network or in underserved areas with limited reticulation.

In Accra, provision is on average better than in most of urban Ghana, and coverage is estimated at 82%. This is likely to be an overestimate, as piped provision is intermittent, not all households in covered areas are actually connected, and many poor communities still rely on secondary and tertiary suppliers for their water needs. As the ground water is saline, wells and boreholes are not a solution for the poor in Accra as in some other cities. This means that SWEs who rely on utility supply are the only suppliers for the poor in Accra.

Types of SWEs and how they operate

In Ghana, the Ghana Water Company (GWC) is the utility mandated to supply water in urban areas. All other secondary and tertiary suppliers of water fall within the category of small water enterprises (SWEs).

The SWEs of Accra comprise the following:
* tanker operators;
* cart operators;
* domestic vendors;
* neighbourhood sellers; and
* sachet water/ice block sellers.

All the above operators obtain water from the utility water system, and form important intermediary supply chains between the utility and the end users. The tanker operators obtain water from specified filling points within the utility's distribution system, and then sell to domestic vendors, and also directly to end users such as households and commercial establishments.

Assessment of supply chains in Accra

The principal supply chains reaching the informal settlements selected in Accra are illustrated in Table 2.6.

Although the SWE supply chains are known to exist, only the relationship between the utility and the water tankers' association is formalised. Through the agreements with the tankers' association, GWC attempts to loosely regulate their operations in the areas of water quality and price. Despite this relationship, the utility does not see most SWEs as a legitimate part of the supply chain, key to meeting the requirements of the unserved and or underserved customers, many of whom are the poor. SWEs are largely seen as exploiters or at best a nuisance to other water consumers, because their activities are perceived as depriving others from getting supplies.

2.6   SWEs and the urban poor in informal settlements in Dar es Salaam, Nairobi, Khartoum and Accra

People who live in informal settlements without piped water networks or other adequate water supplies are poor virtually by definition: they lack the means to meet basic human needs. But even within such settlements there are many different levels and forms of poverty. These differences can, in turn, make a difference to their ability to cope with water deprivation, and to take advantage of the services of SWEs.

Levels of non-access to piped water services are very high across the four cities (and particularly in the low-income areas). The level of piped water provision in the settlements that have been studied is probably representative of the situation faced by many poor people.

Three groups of consumers, with different levels of income poverty, can be discerned among the households surveyed in the four study settlements. These groups relate differently to the SWEs, roughly as follows:
- The highest income group is able to invest in pipes and/or storage facilities, and can buy water in bulk if necessary. In some cases, this group simply meets their own needs. In others, it takes part in water vending, perhaps through the employment of others.
- The middle-income group has sufficient income to purchase water for household needs although it is clearly a struggle to afford sufficient quantities of water. This group buys from a number of sources (minimising costs where possible) and perhaps goes to the extra expense of boiling drinking water to reduce the risk of ill-health and the associated costs. This group is likely to be more dependent

Table 2.6. Supply chains in Accra

Supply chain	Customer
Network→Tanker→Kiosk→Households	~70% of households normally; ~95% in times of shortage
Network→Cart operator→Households	~8% of households normally; ~0% in times of shortage
Network→Kiosk→Cart operator→Households	~20% of households normally; ~5% in times of shortage
Network→Kiosk→Households	~2% of households normally; ~0% in times of shortage

Box 2.2. The Millennium Development Goals and SWEs

The Millennium Development Goals focus on relieving poverty and deprivation, and have a series of about 15 global targets that include:
- By 2015 reduce by half the proportion of people without access to safe drinking water.
- By 2020 achieve significant improvement in the lives of at least 100 million slum dwellers.

Improving and extending the services of SWEs in urban areas could both improve the lives of slum dwellers and improve access to water among currently deprived households. Unfortunately, improved services from water vendors have no effect on the statistics used to monitor whether these targets are being achieved.

The indicator that is being used to monitor progress towards the first of these targets presumes that if a household relies on water vendors, it does not have reasonable access to safe drinking water (WHO and UNICEF 2000). This reflects an inherent problem with using such targets as a guide to action, compounded by a measurement problem specific to vendors. The inherent problem is that targets based on single standards can be used to justify neglecting incremental improvements in the conditions for the worst off, in favour of improvements for those people whose water conditions are already close to acceptable. In the case of vendor users, this problem is compounded by the fact that while it is very easy to discern that a household is using a vendor, it is very difficulty to measure the quality of this provision. Even when household survey results are available, they usually just indicate that a vendor is being used, not the amount or quality of water purchased. Since vendor water is usually expensive and vendor users are usually poor, it is safest to assume that vendor users are not providing acceptable supplies. Unfortunately, this means that no improvements to vendor provision can have any effect on the indicators of progress in reducing the proportion of people without access to safe drinking water.

Yet improving the well-being of the urban poor through SWEs is clearly within the spirit of the Millennium Development Goals. The emphasis that the Goals bring to improving the lives of slum dwellers and to improving water supplies in deprived areas, ought to bring more attention to SWEs. Monitoring and evaluation difficulties must not be allowed to change this.

on small scale water vendors, as households lack the assets needed to invest in improved plot level facilities such as piped water and storage (even where this is a possibility).

• A third group is the very low-income households. These households appear to struggle to afford water, not surprisingly as average expenditure on water appears to be 10 per cent of average income. The very poor try to find additional (free) sources and perhaps buy very small amounts from vendors sufficient for drinking water although not sufficient to ensure good hygiene and health. The personalised relationships between vendors and purchasers help the latter to manage with small payments, and the possibilities of credit facilities (particularly important with highly variable informal incomes) further improve their chance of access.

The poor as consumers
Table 2.7 summarises a poverty analysis for the areas of the cities included in this study highlighting the significance of SWEs.

In Khartoum (the Sudan), two-thirds of the city's population is dependent on groundwater extracted through boreholes and wells and distributed to households by water cart. This percentage rises to 95 to 98 per cent in the informal areas that serve four million of the poorest residents many of which are migrants or internally displaced people fleeing war. In Kenya, more than 60 per cent of the urban poor are supplied by water kiosks and water vendors, rather than directly from the piped network. In Maili Saba (Nairobi, Kenya) itself, 94 per cent of the consumers interviewed are supplied by water vendors (with most of these vendors purchasing from water kiosks with mains connections).

In Accra, coverage for the piped network in Accra-Tema Metropolitan Area appears very high at an estimated 82%, but many poor communities and some others nevertheless rely on secondary and tertiary suppliers for their water supplies (BiG/Adam Smith International 2002). Water is rationed in most areas of Accra city, and especially in areas on the eastern supply network. Some areas only have a supply one or two days in a week and other areas do not get flows for several weeks. In the absence of supplies, vendors play a critical role. 19 of the 28 households interviewed in the study area relied on water vendors. In Dar es Salaam, City Water records (August, 2004) estimate that there are 104,950 connections, of which 95,642 are domestic connections each estimated to serve about 10 people. Hence approximately 1.0 million people (42 per cent) are served by direct connections. Community water supply systems serve an additional 0.1 million people - 4 per cent of the city population (World Bank 2003). Utility water resellers supply about

Table 2.7. Summary of poverty and water supply in the study areas				
	Dar es Salaam	**Nairobi**	**Khartoum**	**Accra**
Average monthly income (estimated for study area)	US$36	US$84	US$152	US$153
Average monthly expenditure on water as percentage of income	13%	9%	9.2%	9.1% typical, not average
Percentage in settlement supplied by SWEs	all but very few	94%	100%	68%
Cost of water from SWE	US$4-6 /m^3	US$ 3.5/m^3 more in shortage	US$ 23.2 /month	Up to US$6/m^3
Cost of piped water	US$0.5 for up to one cubic meter	US$1.4/m^3	US$0.6 /month	US$0.5/m^3

Conversion rates employed: US$1 equals 1136 Tanzania shillings, 73.4 Kenyan shillings, 258.5 Sudanese dinars, 9110 Ghanaian cedis (www.economist.com 26/03/05)

35 per cent of residents, tanker trucks about 2 per cent, pushcart vendors 2 per cent and private and communal boreholes 13 per cent. An estimated 2 per cent of water used is secured from unprotected sources (surface sources are not used much because they are polluted). Thus the total percentage coverage through various vendors is estimated at over half of the population.

Water is used for meeting basic needs and livelihood activities with different sources being used for different activities. In Maili Saba (Nairobi), for example, water from the utility, kiosks and vendors is mainly used for construction, cooking, drinking, washing utensils/clothes and brewing alcohol. Well water is mainly used to clean houses and latrines, bathing, washing and sometimes cooking. Some use it for sprinkling on the earth floor to limit dust. Borehole water is used for brewing alcohol, cooking, washing, bathing and drinking. Spring water is used for washing, cooking and sometimes drinking. Water from roof catchments is used for cooking, bathing, washing, drinking. Water choice is differentiated by activity and different sources are selected for different water uses. In Nairobi, respondents recognise that drinking water uses the least amount of water but the respondents rated it as the highest need requiring the best quality. Fifty-nine per cent of the respondents boil their drinking water (incurring additional costs), implying that they perceived water quality to be poor. The livelihood water uses in Sandali (Dar es Salaam) are divided into domestic water use (water for drinking, cooking, bathing and cleaning of cooking utensils, house cleaning and cloth washing) and for informal and formal micro enterprises use (informal food kiosks, local brewers, guest houses and restaurants). Water for drinking and cooking is usually collected from sources with water that tastes good; namely from utility pipe sources or from privately owned boreholes, community managed boreholes or community managed utility kiosks. Water for the other uses is often collected from boreholes or shallow well sources with salty water.

The significance of the role of women in water-related activities is notable in a number of countries. In Maili Saba, women are responsible for 73 per cent of decisions about purchasing in terms of water source and quantity. In Khartoum, women and girls are also responsible for water provision to their households.

Despite very low incomes in the settlements studied, costs of water appear relatively high with a remarkably consistent percentage of incomes (between 9-13 per cent) being allocated to water purchase. Earlier studies in the same cities have produced similar or higher expenditures; for example, in the poorest areas of Khartoum, households spend between 17 and 25 per cent of income on water for domestic use.

Income and asset shortages mean that households have very limited choices and this is the context in which they use SWEs. In Accra, a socio-economic survey undertaken on behalf of the Public Utilities Regulatory Commission (PURC) showed that connection fees are indeed a barrier to access for low-income households, with 28 per cent of those surveyed citing that as a barrier to access (Adam Smith International 2002). From 1999 to 2002, over 15 per cent of average annual household income (41 per cent in 2002) was required to be connected to the utility's mains. Two other examples also indicate the difficulties faced by households in raising sufficient income to secure water supplies. In Accra, low-income households are attracted to the informal providers because they offer credit; 37 per cent of low-income respondents have used this facility with most settling as soon as possible. In Nairobi, despite chronic water shortage, most consumers have not been able to invest in water storage facilities (enabling them to purchase more when prices are lower) due to financial constraints.

In every city, SWE prices are high compared to those for piped water. In Dar es Salaam, the majority of households without piped water in Mwembeladu and Sandali and in the other three sub-wards usually buy water from street vendors, or directly from private or community managed boreholes. The purchase price at the source ranges from US$0.45 – 0.75/ m^3 and the sale price ranges from US$4.0 – 6.3/ m^3 which is about 8 times the purchase price. The sale price per 20 litre jerrycan which is charged by the street water vendors ranges between US$3.0 – 4.4/ m^3. The purchase price at the source ranges between US$0.9 – 1.3/ m^3.

The higher purchase price of US$1.3/ m³ is charged by borehole owners during periods of public power supply interruptions in which case the borehole operator uses a private standby power generator to ensure continuity of water supply to customers.

The costs of provision and the implications for the poorest

The high cost of water makes it difficult for the poorest to afford to purchase sufficient supplies. In Khartoum, the poorest households walk to the water yards and collect water directly rather than paying water cart operators to deliver to their homes. About 5 per cent of residents in informal settlements are estimated to use this strategy to reduce their water costs. Proximity to a water yard enables direct collection especially by children, who do not have to pay for small quantities. In Kenya, the poorer households develop coping mechanisms for supplying water for household use. These include self-collecting water instead of buying from vendors, collecting water from unprotected sources for some chores (washing) and reducing the amount of water used. These households are extremely vulnerable during shortage. (Other households boil their drinking water as a means of improving quality with the inherent increased fuel costs, usually charcoal.)

In Accra, one coping strategy observed was that in almost one in five of houses in Teshie practice water vending. When there is water shortage the vendors sell only to a certain level and keep the rest of the water for their family and neighbours who are close and regular customers. This ensures that even in very difficult times, they will still have access to water for their domestic use. However, it is not evident that this strategy is available to the poorest households. When water becomes difficult and expensive to access, poor households along the coast (including Old Teshie) use the sea for bathing, for example. In Dar es Salaam, the people who cannot afford water supply charges use the nearby unsafe traditional river water source (Yombo river) and hand dug wells in the riverbed especially for water for washing and cleaning purposes. The respondents said cholera and other diseases like diarrhoea and dysentery are endemic in the area, and attributed these diseases to unsafe water supply sources including the Yombo River. The quality of this river water is generally unfit for any household use.

The role of SWEs as employment opportunities

As noted already, water vending is a livelihood strategy for the poor. Some of the poor are water sellers as well as users. Buying in large volumes reduces the price of water.

Table 2.8 summarises information about water vendors in the four study settlements.

Table 2.8. Characteristics of water vending and water vendors in Dar es Salaam, Nairobi, Khartoum and Accra				
	Dar es Salaam	**Nairobi**	**Khartoum**	**Accra**
Age	18-30	50% less than 30	12-35	No information
Sex	Mainly men	Half men and half women, with the women carrying rather than using bicycles	Male	Generally women, but men for driving tankers and carts
Incomes	-	US$ 25-74 /month	US$50-125 /month	US$ 120 /month
Problems	Health problems due to carrying and pushing cart	High operating costs due to repairs and replacements of the plastic water containers that they use. Competition	Authority harassment	High competition for water, poor market in wet season

Conversion rates employed: US$1 equals 1136 Tanzania shillings, 73.4 Kenyan shillings, 258.5 Sudanese dinars, 9110 Ghanaian cedis (www.economist.com, 26/03/05)

The activity appears to be a viable commercial enterprise for those living in low-income settlements with daily incomes ranging from just under US $ 1 to 5 across the three cities for which information is available. At the lower end, this is likely to be similar to informal unskilled wages in other sectors. Generally vendors are young, reflecting the physical nature of the activity. In some cases, vendors own their assets but in other circumstances this seems difficult and they are dependent on higher income residents to make the required investment. Hence:

• In Maili Saba, Nairobi, the total cost of setting up a water kiosk varies from about US$ 150 to over US $ 950 depending on the length of the pipeline to be installed. The procedures are reported to be cumbersome and often require bribes. These procedures are not displayed on public notice boards, thus are not easily accessible to the applicants. Starting water kiosks is cumbersome and thus very few persons have ventured in that direction. However, there is now an increase in bicycle and backload vendors competing for the same and shrinking market. For the bicycle vendors the start-up consists of purchase of a bicycle and some 20 litre jerrycans for carrying the water. Currently they are not required to obtain any licence from the water/city authorities. The backload carriers only need to buy containers and start the business. The main sources of funds for starting the business include remittances by family/relatives (53%), individual savings (34%), retirement benefits (10%) and micro financing (3%).

- In Khartoum, 80 per cent of vendors in "Dar Al Salam" informal settlement own donkey carts; the other 20 per cent access the donkey carts via profit sharing mechanisms with their owners.
- In Accra the lack of an effective piped network means that tankers are significant suppliers of water to local vendors. In effect, there is a high degree of inter-dependence and the key customers of the tankers are the vendors who account for 85 percent of their 1st ranked customers.

Chapter 3

The constraints on and opportunities for SWEs to improve water provision

For many years SWEs were considered to be operators who exploited the poor, selling water of dubious quality at vastly inflated prices to vulnerable poor communities. This perception caused animosity between SWEs and water utility staff, and discouraged dialogue between them. The negative image of SWEs hindered initiatives to improve water provision, and continues to be a constraint to improving services.

More recently, studies have shown that SWEs do not deserve their reputation for exploiting the poor. Studies on SWEs in Khartoum have shown that SWE's margins are low, so it is not SWEs who are exploiting the poor (Albu and Njiru 2002). Indeed, the prices charged for water by SWEs are not necessarily excessive for the service provided, the quality of water supplied by SWEs is often similar to that supplied by the local utility, and SWEs often provide services that are valued by their customers. Customers often benefit from a personal relationship with an SWE. Changes in perception provide opportunities for SWEs to enjoy more respect, and in some cities to enter into discussions with water utility staff to create partnerships that could improve water supply for the poor.

Governments and water utilities remain hesitant about engaging with SWEs. This is not surprising. Working with SWEs can seem to present authorities and utilities with a no-win situation. If they support water vendors they risk being seen to condone a system wherein the better off receive piped water connections while the worse off receive services that are more expensive and less convenient. But if they suppress water vendors the (black market) price of vended water goes up still further, amplifying the inequalities. Similarly, the government and the utility are likely to be blamed if even a small minority of SWEs sell contaminated water, but are also likely to be blamed if their regulations drive SWEs out of business and lead to higher prices. Hence, there is need for a strategy on the part of the utility for progressive integration and/or regulation of SWEs into the utility's supply chain.

This reticence on the part of utilities and authorities is one of the obstacles that need to be overcome in order to tap the full potential of SWEs. Governments cannot be responsible for everything that SWEs do. On the other hand, they can and should be responsible for the rules under which SWEs operate, and the measures taken to enforce these rules. Similarly, utilities cannot be responsible for the price, quality or quantity of water that SWEs deliver. But they can and should be made responsible for providing services to SWEs, when this is likely to be a cost effective way of improving water provision in deprived neighbourhoods. Care clearly needs to be taken to ensure that by working with SWEs, governments and utilities do not lose their incentive to extend the piped water system. As already noted, however, incremental improvements are likely to be central to improving water provision in informal settlements for many years to come.

Following a brief summary of the constraints and opportunities associated with SWEs generally, the rest of this report examines the constraints and opportunities found in the four cities studied.

Overall, the assessment of constraints and opportunities indicates that:
- the SWE-based water systems fulfil a critically important role, especially in informal settlements;
- they do not function as well as they could, however, and face a number of unnecessary constraints (as well as inherent limitations);
- many of these constraints stem from dysfunctional relations between the more formal government and utility managed water system and the less formal SWE managed systems;
- in all of the cities, political, legal or policy changes are providing opportunities to improve these relations;
- if these opportunities are seized, currently deprived residents should benefit from more reliable and less expensive water supplies, and in most cases utilities should benefit from a larger customer base; and
- achieving better relations will require hard work, and learning by doing.

Constraints
In different locations, SWEs face a variety of constraints, both local and general. Literature suggests that some problems faced by SWEs may include:
- difficulties in obtaining licences to operate the water business;
- difficulties in obtaining permission from local power-brokers (cartels);

- technical difficulties related to water sources and transportation; and
- vandalism of competitors' installations to discourage competition from new entrants.

The research in Tanzania, Kenya, Sudan and Ghana provided examples of some, but not all, of these. The research in these countries found no evidence of cartels, although Snell (1998) refers to 'mastans' in Dhaka, Bangladesh, using their power to maintain a monopoly on water supply, and charging high prices. Snell (1998) also refers to examples of rivalry between SWEs in Kibera (Nairobi, Kenya) and Lima (Peru), with the rivalry sometimes resulting in deliberate damage to competitors' property.

Regulations may constrain some SWEs, who may lack awareness of licensing issues. Depending on the location, SWEs (whether licensed or unlicensed) may face harassment from local officials, or unlicensed SWEs may only encounter problems if the scale of the operation is increased. Utilities may not seek redress against SWEs who operate illegally, and may charge SWEs commercial rates for their water, even if water selling is illegal. Other constraints that may affect SWE activities include:
- limited access to water supplies. SWE operations may be constrained because of inefficient utility management in aspects such as the reliability of water supplies, and billing arrangements;
- lack of co-ordination among SWEs. Some areas may be served by several SWEs, while other areas may be poorly served;
- frequent lack of access to financial credit;
- lack of relevant skills for business management;
- some customers and water utilities continue in the perception that SWEs are dishonest, selling water of poor quality at inflated prices; and
- limited dialogue and co-operation between SWEs and utilities.

Opportunities

SWEs have already taken advantage of local opportunities. They are often enterprising, able to identify innovative local solutions to water supply problems. In areas where SWEs obtain water from intermittent or unreliable utility water supplies, some SWEs may be able to construct tanks to store water so that they are able to continue supplying water during periods of interrupted flow.

SWEs generally have freedom to adopt a flexible pricing policy. Not all water used domestically needs to be of potable quality, and a flexible pricing policy may give SWEs the freedom to meet different niches in the local domestic water market. Prices may depend on factors such as water availability, water quality, and customer loyalty.

SWEs often enjoy a regular and reliable market, with demand for their services, especially where utility water is limited. They are known and accepted by the communities in which they work, and they generally provide useful services that complement utility services.

In some places such as Accra, SWEs are now recognised by utilities, and some SWEs have formed local associations to provide mutual support, to strengthen their negotiating position, and to co-ordinate their activities. Regulation, whether official or self-imposed, may in some situations provide opportunities for setting and maintaining standards of service, for example in aspects such as water price and quality.

Better relations between SWEs and the formal water authorities and managers provide opportunities for both sides to improve water provisioning. By recognising and building on the role of SWEs, utilities can adopt policies and undertake investments that take explicit account of how SWEs will use the water made available to them, and how government policy and utility planning affect local water market outcomes. SWEs can gain access to better water supplies, and potentially to the finance required to invest in better technologies.

3.1   Constraints and opportunities in Dar es Salaam

In Dar es Salaam, most of the urban poor live in informal settlements with limited or no utility water networks. Where networks exist, the flow of water is often intermittent. Utility water coverage through direct connections is estimated at 42 per cent, which implies that about 58% of consumers receive water through a supply chain in which SWEs play a pivotal role. Kiosks and itinerant vendors are especially important in the study area. Those segments of the water supply chain controlled by SWEs have two salient features:
- They are privately or community controlled, and the SWEs are motivated by either profit incentives and competition pressures (for privately controlled chains), or social objectives (for community controlled chains), or both.
- They are rarely fully legitimate, in that most SWEs are not properly registered, use utility water without payment, or fail basic quality standards.

Despite their questionable legitimacy, most SWEs have the following strengths:
- They supply an important market, that is not served by the water utility.
- They are accepted within the local community because their services are valued.

- They provide employment to itinerant vendors and kiosk attendants in the settlements.
- The itinerant water vendors operate in highly competitive conditions, and have very little opportunity to secure excess profits.
- The kiosk operators have a good understanding of the local water market, and have experience of operating commercial establishments in difficult conditions.
- SWEs have been recognised by the revised National Water Policy, increasing their potential legitimacy.

While kiosks and itinerant vendors already play a critical role, their supply chains remain highly constrained, and there are numerous opportunities for improvement. Institutional and technical improvements could lead to lower costs, reduced prices, higher quality water, and more regular supplies. Some of the most important improvements could be achieved through better relations between the utility and the SWEs. The utility has better access to water, technologies and even finance. Combining their strengths, the utility and the SWEs could greatly improve water provisioning in the informal settlements of Dar es Salaam. There is still some uncertainty, however, concerning how these strengths are best combined in practice, and in particular the extent to which the utility and the government need to regulate as well as facilitate the operations of the SWEs.

The itinerant vendors operate in highly competitive conditions, but the water supplies available to the kiosks are limited and of variable quality. The main water sources for the kiosks are:
- private boreholes;
- community boreholes; and
- the utility's distribution network.

Water from private and community boreholes is said to be of variable quality. For instance, the water is often saline. Until recently (see below), the utility has not engaged with SWEs, limiting supplies from the utility's piped water network into the SWE markets. This created a situation where the legality of all SWEs was questionable, making it very difficult for customers or the utility to push for improvements, and making it difficult for SWEs to gain access to the finance needed to implement improvements.

Of late, the positive role played by SWEs in serving the poor in Dar es Salaam has begun to be recognised by the utility. Indeed, part of the proposed improvements for water services to the urban poor involves installation of 250 agency operated

kiosks in areas which are currently under-served or unserved by the utility. The intention is for these kiosks to help address several of the constraints kiosks typically face, including:
- availability of water sources;
- lack of adequate investment funds;
- access to technical and financial assistance; and
- water quality.

The utility and some customers support the establishment of utility kiosks that would deliver water to households and street water vendors at a controlled price. Some officials are concerned that the provision of water by SWEs should not be encouraged because it is difficult to control prices and water quality, especially for street water vendors. On the other hand, working with SWEs in the informal settlements is one way of tapping the financial and human resources of the local private sector into the water sector. Moreover, excessive regulations controlling water prices and quality could suppress supplies, and favour illegitimate markets.

Discussions between various stakeholders have already resulted in the recognition and increased acceptance of SWEs. The utility has agreed to install limited but key pipelines to supply pilot kiosks with utility water. Different management arrangements will be piloted, with a view to establishing functional models for setting up and managing SWE operated kiosks in partnership with the water utility. The economic competitiveness and public benefits of these partnerships can then be ascertained. The result of this intervention is likely to lead to one or more of the following:
- greater SWE business legality and contractual formality (hence lower SWE costs from rent-seeking and related evasion strategies, and better access to finance for SWE investment);
- more technically efficient water delivery systems (pipes, storage, kiosks, vending etc) that lower overall costs along the SWE water supply chain sufficiently to justify Utility or SWE investment;
- more effective systems for Utility revenue collection (that would not be practicable without collaboration of SWEs);
- new ways of protecting and policing the infrastructure and water resources of both Utility and SWEs to reduce damage and water losses for both parties;
- more effective ways for poor water consumers to express and get redress in respect of their concerns e.g. about exploitative prices, quality or shortages etc; and

- more effective ways for SWEs to express and get redress in respect of their concerns e.g. about barriers to entry, rent-seeking, supply pressures and continuity, excessive business risks etc.

3.2   Constraints and opportunities in Nairobi

Almost all residents and businesses in informal settlements like Maili Saba (which is broadly representative of other informal settlements in Nairobi) depend on water supply chains in which SWEs - i.e. private kiosks, and to a lesser extent manual vendors - play a critical role.

These chains have two salient features, similar to those in Dar es Salaam:
- They are privately-controlled, so the kiosk owners and other vendors are motivated by profit incentives and have to cope with, or suppress, competitive pressures.
- They are not fully legitimate. Kiosk owners in particular frequently have substandard, illegal or dubiously arranged connections to the utility's mains supply.

The supply-chain involving NCWSCL's water and private kiosks clearly works, but not nearly as well as it could in terms of costs incurred, prices charged, regularity and quality of water supplied to poor urban consumers. Revenue collection is haphazard; quality is not assured, supply is constrained and unreliable.

The research indicates, in particular, that the lack of transparency and unclear legality involved in setting up private kiosk connections to NCWSCL discourages new entrants in the water services market; is a disincentive for kiosk operators to invest in their businesses adequately; creates opportunities for rent-seeking; deprives NCWSCL of revenue; contributes to water losses from sub-standard private pipelines, and thus adds to the overall cost of water for consumers.

This dysfunctional interface between the NCWSCL-controlled and the SWE-controlled (ie. kiosks, manual vendors) sections of the water chain is a major problem. It creates high transaction costs and risks, discourages investment for both parties, and blocks new kiosk entrants. As a result neither the NCWSCL delivery system, nor the private water services market work well.

However, the current political context in each city creates an environment in which there are new opportunities for changing this. In particular the privatisation of Nairobi City Council water services means that there are now new regulatory and political incentives to reduce unaccounted for water, improve revenue collection and improve quality of services in informal settlements. The privatised water utility (NCWSCL) has already embarked in 2005 on a specific initiative in the Mukuru area settlements of eastern Nairobi aimed at reducing water losses, improving revenue collection, regularising connections and streamlining the procedures for obtaining connections at the NCWSCL offices.

We anticipate that unquantifiable but potentially large benefits could emerge from improving this interface between the NCWSCL and SWE-controlled sections of the water chain.

The benefits could fall into the following categories:
- **Consumer convenience**
  Reducing entry barriers into the water services market would lead to an increase in the density of water kiosks in the settlements, making for shorter average household distances to water points, and shorter queues for water.
- **Lower prices**
  More reliable connections, better in-settlement infrastructure and greater competition between kiosk operators would lead to lower prices. It could especially reduce the very high surcharges that occur during water shortages.
- **Technical upgrading**
  Regularising both the physical connections and the contractual arrangements with kiosk owners, opens up the potential to upgrade substandard pipelines within the settlement and improve kiosk outlets. This will improve water quality and reduce water losses.
- **Increased net revenue for NCWSCL**
  Currently only a tiny proportion of the average monthly household expenditure on water (US$ 7) is returned to the NCWSCL. Regularising the contractual arrangements with kiosk owners will lead to increased legitimate revenue collection for the NCWSCL, and reduce rent-seeking by water officials and other local power-brokers.

Specific opportunities for improving access to water in the Nairobi settlements revolve around the following initiatives or developments:
- **Greater SWE business legality and contractual formality**
  The NCWSCL initiative to regularise kiosk connections in informal settlements involves establishing secure, metered housings (connection chambers) for connecting kiosk owners. These customers would be recognised as legitimate partners in water delivery, with appropriate and enforceable contractual arrangements.

Greater business legitimacy for kiosk owners may make it easier and less risky for them to secure finance for investing in kiosk infrastructure (e.g. storage, pipes), and to resist rent-seeking activity. The major challenge will be to devise contractual arrangements and monitoring mechanisms that protect kiosk owners from extortion, and discourage them from forming price-fixing cartels.

- **More technically efficient water delivery systems that lower overall costs along the water supply chain sufficiently to justify NCWSCL or private kiosk investment**

  The proposed connection chambers could contribute to the upgrading of the minor pipelines that reticulate water to kiosks and water points within the settlements. By locating the chambers (connection points) closer to the centre of settlements, the length of pipeline required for reticulating individual kiosks will be lowered. Also by making the kiosk owners responsible for water losses between meter chamber and their outlets, the incentives for investing in, and maintaining, pipelines of a reasonable standard will be greatly enhanced. However kiosk owners will need effective mechanisms for protecting this investment against illicit connections and vandalism.

- **More effective systems for NCWSCL revenue collection**

  The regularisation of kiosk businesses as NCWSCL customers, using secure meter chambers owned by NCWSCL, offers an opportunity for NCWSCL to significantly increase its revenue and reduce unaccounted-for-water. The greatest advantage to NCWSCL stems from shifting responsibility for cost of water losses downstream of the meter chambers (i.e. within the informal settlements) onto the shoulders of the kiosk operators. This will be reinforced by greater NCWSCL control over the supply and ease of disconnections in the event of arrears.

- **New ways of protecting and policing the infrastructure and water resources of both NCWSCL and kiosk operators to reduce damage and unaccounted losses for both parties**

  The secure meter chamber initiative offers NCWSCL a way of protecting and policing its own water resources. However this will only improve performance of the overall water chain (ie. deliver benefits to consumers) if kiosk operators also have practicable mechanisms for policing "their" pipes – that is detecting water losses and preventing theft or loss of water. NCWSCL will need to find ways to support the kiosk owners to do this, or they will find that no kiosk owners sign up to be supplied by the new system.

- **More effective ways for poor water consumers to express and get redress in respect of their concerns e.g. about exploitative prices, quality or shortages**

  In a more regularised relationship, NCWSCL will need to take some responsibility for preventing price-fixing cartels among kiosk operators, and excessive surcharging during supply shortages. Retail price caps may be appropriate. It may be necessary to reserve some connections for community-managed kiosks. NCWSCL may need to set enforceable guidelines for acceptable levels of service provided by kiosk operators. Water consumers (civil society) will need to be provided with mechanisms for expressing concerns and getting redress in case of uncompetitive behaviour by kiosk owners.

- **More effective ways for kiosk owners to express and get redress in respect of their concerns e.g. about barriers to entry, rent-seeking, supply pressures and continuity, excessive business risks**
  Price-fixing and other uncompetitive practices can result from criminal activities that target kiosk operators (e.g. sunk investment in kiosk infrastructure makes them vulnerable to blackmail). Because NCWSCL has a monopoly on supply, kiosk operators are also vulnerable to policies and arbitrary actions by NCWSCL (such as supply failures) that might render their businesses unprofitable. It will be necessary, therefore, to create mechanisms that give kiosk owners protection or redress. An association of kiosk owners – provided it does not encourage price-fixing itself – might play this role.

3.3 Constraints and opportunities in Khartoum

In Khartoum's peri-urban areas, some 80 per cent of the population get water through a supply chain in which SWEs play a pivotal role - in the form of donkey cart operators and also privately managed water yards. Donkey cart operators are entirely independent SWEs, motivated by profit incentives and competition pressures. Although recognised and tolerated by officials, most work at the fringes of legality, due to burdensome public health licensing, taxes and their use of some "unsafe" water sources. Although most water yards are owned by KSWC, their performance is inadequate and the state-owned utility is already experimenting with community and private management arrangements.

The water yard supply chain does function, but not nearly as well as it could, in terms of costs incurred, prices charged, and the regularity and quality of water supplied to poor urban consumers. Intense competition exists between cart operators, but other institutional characteristics of the water system are creating problems, and these problems are reflected in the quality and price of service delivery.

A major problem seems to be the dysfunctional interrelations between the cart-operators and the KSWC-controlled water yards. These create very high transaction costs and risks for the cart operators, and discourage investment by both parties.

As a result neither the water yard delivery system, nor the private water services market involving cart operators and consumers, work well.

The dysfunctionality of the Utility – SWE interface in Khartoum has three aspects:
- institutional weaknesses in KSWC;
- water yard management problems; and
- restrictions on cart operators.

The institutional weaknesses in KSWC take three forms. First, there is a management and professional bias towards meeting the needs of KSWC's network-connected customers; providing water to SWEs is seen as a secondary concern. For example, priority is given to renovating and expanding the Nile extraction and treatment infrastructure, and the needs of the peri-urban settlements that rely on boreholes are neglected. Second, like all Sudanese public institutions, KSWC struggles to retain qualified technical staff, particularly engineers, and therefore has inadequate capacity to service and maintain the water yards. Third, political caution and bureaucratic inertia make the KSWC slow to explore innovative or alternative solutions such as licensing of water yard management to private contractors.

Water yard management problems are also critical. At any time up to one third of yards are inoperative – usually due to lack of spare parts or technical support to repair pumps. This increases delivery costs significantly. Active yards have little incentive to improve efficiency and this is evident in their operations – particularly in the organisation of cart filling. Cart operators often spend two or three hours a day queuing, with significant cost implications for consumers. In addition, many water yards have very poor drainage and sanitation arrangements, with public health implications.

Cart operators face additional constraints, principally associated with licensing requirements. There are five different licences or permits needed, and enforcement of each provides opportunities for rent-seeking by low paid officials. Confiscation of carts is routine. Other constraints reflect crude, but low-cost technologies used for construction of the water tanks and donkey carts. These mean that tanks are unhygienic and carts cause unnecessary injury to the animals. Cart operators lack access to financial services to invest in better equipment, or may have little incentive due to their lack of ownership of assets.

Although there are an estimated 30,000 to 40,000 water cart operators in Greater Khartoum, there is no effective association to represent their interests or articulate their needs. Operators have low self-esteem and mistrust the authorities (in water and health departments) who should be working with them.

However, the current political context in Khartoum does create an environment in which there are new opportunities for changing this situation. The State government and KSWC are coming under increasing political pressure to provide a better water service for the population living in the peri-urban zones, some parts of which are finally being recognised as permanent settlements. KSWC management at the highest level is beginning to appreciate the importance of SWEs, and the need to work with SWEs if they are to improve services beyond the piped network. In addition, there appears to be greater acceptance of the potential positive role that private entrepreneurs could play in managing (if not owning) water yards.

We anticipate unquantifiable but potentially very large benefits from improving water yard investment and management, and the interface between water yards and cart operators in particular.

The benefits fall into the following categories:
- **Consumer convenience**
  Better water yard management and greater investment could significantly reduce the average household distance to a functioning water point (e.g. from 2 km to less than 1 km) with major benefits to almost all households regardless of how they procure water.
- **Lower prices**
  Variable costs related to the water-hauling distance and the waiting time at water yards account for as much as half the operating costs of cart operators. Reducing distances and filling delays could therefore cut retail prices significantly, especially since there is healthy competition between cart operators.
- **Technical upgrading**
  Investment in water yard layout and hygiene would reduce public health risks associated with the process of filling donkey cart tanks. Less hostile official behaviour towards cart operators, and greater income security, could also encourage investment in more hygienic carts and water tanks.
- **Increased net revenue for utility**
  In principle, lower retail prices for water (above) and greater convenience of access should encourage greater volume consumption. The revenue raised by KSWC should therefore increase proportionately – hopefully offsetting the costs of investment in water yards.

Specific opportunities for improving access to water in the settlements revolve around these initiatives or developments:

Greater SWE business legality and contractual formality, and more effective ways for SWEs to express and get redress in respect of their concerns

- Cart operators could be assisted to form association(s) to represent their needs and negotiate with KSWC and the Department of Health. The aim should be to improve water yards, rationalise licensing procedures, reduce rent-seeking activities and improve their access to finance for investment in carts, tanks etc. Challenges will include bridging the ethnic, cultural and social gulf that separates cart operators from public officials.

More technically efficient water delivery systems

- The performance of water yards (in terms of throughput) could be significantly improved by KSWC investing in pumps, cart loading facilities, drainage and other works. The costs would be much lower than work on prestigious new surface water extraction and treatment plant. The major challenge will be to win support from KSWC officials for such a low-visibility low-status initiative.
- The performance of water yards (in terms of reliability) could be improved by greatly expanding experimental arrangements for licensing private water yard management agents. The challenge will be to devise a pricing or incentive structure that motivates these agent to maximise water yard performance, and makes proper maintenance and timely repair of water yard equipment (e.g. pumps) a rational investment.
- Low cost, improved technologies of water tank and donkey cart manufacture should be market tested – with the aim of improving hygiene, reducing weight, increasing resilience and improving animal health. The major challenge will be to devise attractive financing mechanisms so that cart operators can invest in new equipment.

3.4   Constraints and opportunities in Accra

SWEs in Accra range from the numerous households that sell water to their neighbours to strategically important water tankers that transport water from one part of the city to another. As in the other cities, SWEs in Accra have historically existed at the boundaries of legality, and although they play an important role, they face many constraints and do not contribute as much as they could to addressing Accra's water problems. Relations between the utility and the water tanker operators have improved, however, and the tanker operators have been allowed to join associations. There is still considerable scope for improvement.

Supply related constraints: Although the utility is now engaging with Tanker Operators' associations, the utility has imposed restrictions on the number of days and hours that tankers can operate. There are insufficient points within the distribution system where tankers can fill up, with the result that there are long waiting times for tankers; hence fewer trips and thus inability for tanker operators to meet water supply requirements of vendors and consumers, creating shortages and high end-user prices. Lack of alternative supply sources outside the utility is limiting the scope of SWE operations. By engaging more positively with SWEs, the utility can develop more filling points for tankers, to enable them to better play their role in meeting the water requirements of those who rely on them for their supply.

Pricing constraints: The utility charges Tanker Operators a commercial tariff that is well above the domestic tariff. Tanker prices to downstream vendors typically comprise the commercial tariff (paid to the utility), transportation, income tax paid by tankers, and the Tanker Operator's profit. This cost structure translates into higher tanker bulk prices, which in turn results in higher vendor retail prices charged to end users. Although the utility has set tariffs that Tanker Operators should charge to customers, Tanker Operators typically charge their customers 10 - 15 percent above the rates mutually agreed with the utility. Given that the utility's network does not meet the requirements of all end users, a more flexible tariff for Tanker Operators could result in more favourable charges to the end users supplied through the SWEs supply chain.

Water quality constraints: In general, water quality awareness is generally low among the Tanker Operators and their customers. Quality assurance procedures along the SWE supply-chain are non-existent. For downstream vendors, the only means of assessing the quality of water supplied by the tankers is through observing colour, odour and taste of the water. There are no guidelines on ensuring the quality of water delivered by tankers, though the regulator, PURC, is reportedly taking a pro-active role in developing guidelines for water quality. In conjunction with technical support (for transportation and storage of water), water quality guidelines could improve the service provided by SWEs.

Financing constraints: The initial investment for vehicles to be converted into water tankers is high. Credit facilities are unavailable to many SWEs, and this presents a challenge for entry into the business as well in their operations. One of the results is that most of the water tankers used in Accra are very old (some 20 years old), with high breakdown rate and maintenance costs. Development of better financing mechanisms for SWEs could make newer vehicles more economic and improve their operations.

Technology and innovation: In Accra, Tanker Operators typically supply water to vendors, most of whom store the water in underground water tanks. Underground storage presents a challenge to water quality assurance, due to difficulties in cleaning and disinfecting the tanks. The mechanism of bailing water out of these tanks (using buckets) also increases the risk of contamination. Technical support in terms of more efficient storage, or methods of bailing out the water, could improve, or assure, water quality.

Management capacity: SWEs, especially vendors, do not keep proper records and therefore have difficulty assessing the profit margins, especially where they do not separate sales from their own domestic usage. Training in these areas could improve the operation of SWEs.

Recognition: The role of SWEs is not formally recognised, and many operators state that they can play their roles more adequately if given proper recognition and support. Perhaps if SWE operations were properly mainstreamed into the utility's distribution chain, their activities could be regulated and they would have a greater obligation to moderate their charges.

Opportunities: In Accra, opportunities would involve SWEs in obtaining their own water source. This is because there is a general deficit of water supply that affects both formal and informal settlements in all parts of the city. The water utility now recognises the complementary service offered by SWEs, and their association is in discussion with the utility to facilitate use of SWEs as part of the water utility supply chain.

Chapter 4

Concluding remarks

The challenge of achieving the Millennium Development Goals is enormous. Many people living in urban areas of low-income countries currently lack access to safe drinking water, and depend on small water enterprises (SWEs) for their water supplies. SWEs are likely to remain important suppliers of water, especially to the urban poor, for the foreseeable future.

The pace of urbanisation in many low-income countries continues to outstrip the ability of water utilities to provide services for new customers, or even to maintain service standards for existing customers. In many urban areas, network water supplies are already intermittent or inadequate, and there is little prospect for urban water distribution systems to expand quickly enough to keep pace with population increases.

Various different types of SWEs exist in many countries, responding to local conditions and filling niche markets for the supply of water. In many cities, SWEs account for a greater share of the water market than the official utilities, and they often provide services that are valued by their customers. SWEs have acquired a negative image, and this has hindered initiatives to improve water provision, and continues to be a constraint to improving services. Utilities have historically ignored or suppressed SWEs, and the interface between a water utility and local SWEs is a major source of problems in many urban areas of low-income countries. Improving relationships between SWEs and utilities therefore provides an opportunity for realising unquantifiable but potentially very large benefits in the water supply sector.

If water utilities could engage with SWEs, some of the major constraints currently experienced by SWEs could be alleviated or reduced. Collaboration between utilities and SWEs would be to the benefit of customers, thus enabling SWEs to contribute to achieving the Millennium Development Goals that relate to people lacking access to safe drinking water.

References

Adam Smith International (2002), *Socio-economic survey on water accessibility in Ghana*, Public Utilities Regulatory Commission, Accra.

Albu, M. and Njiru, C. (2002), The role of small-scale independent water providers in urban areas", *Waterlines international journal of appropriate technologies for water supply and sanitation*, Vol 20, No 3, pages 14-16.

Ballesteros, M. M. (2002), *Rethinking institutional reforms in the Philippine housing sector*, Discussion Paper Series 2002-16, Philippine Institute for Development Studies, Metro Manila.

Budds, J. and McGranahan, G. (2003), Are the debates on water privatization missing the point? Experiences from Africa, Asia and Latin America, *Environment and Urbanization*, Vol 15, No 2, pages 87-113.

Cairncross, S. and Kinnear, J. (1991), Water vending in urban Sudan, *Water Resources Development*, Vol 7, No 4, pages 267-273.

Conan, H. (2003), *Scope and Scale of Small Scale Independent Private Water Providers in 8 Asian Cities*, Asian Development Bank, Manila.

ESCAP (1991), *Guidelines on Community Based Housing Finance and Innovative Credit Systems for Low-income Households*, Report ST/ESCAP/1003, United Nations Economic and Social Commission for Asia and the Pacific, Bangkok.

Ferguson, B. (2004), Scaling up housing micro-finance: a guide to practice, *Housing Finance International*, Vol 19, No 1, pages 3-13.

Finger, M. and Allouche, J. (2002), *Water Privatisation: Trans-National Corporations and the Re-Regulation of the Water Industry*, Spon Press, London.

REFERENCES

Government of Tanzania and UN-Habitat (2003), *Re-establishing Effective Housing Finance Mechanisms in Tanzania: The Potentials and the Bottlenecks*, UN-Habitat, Nairobi.

Khan, H.R. and Siddique, Q. I. (2000), Urban water management problems in developing countries with particular reference to Bangladesh, *Water Resources Development*, Vol 16, No 1, pages 21-33.

Kjellén, M. and McGranahan, G. (2004), *Informal Water Vendors and Getting Better Services for the Urban Poor*, Thematic Paper for the Urban Forum in Barcelona, UN-Habitat, Nairobi.

McGranahan, G. and Owen, D. L. (2004), *Getting Local Water and Sanitation Companies to Improve Water and Sanitation Provision for the Urban Poor*, Thematic Paper for the Urban Forum in Barcelona, UN-Habitat, Nairobi.

Okpala, D. (1994), Financing housing in developing countries: a review of the pitfalls and potentials in the development of formal housing finance systems, *Urban Studies*, Vol 31, No 9, pages 1571-1586.

Snell, S. (1998), *Water and Sanitation Services for the Urban Poor - Small-Scale Providers: Typology & Profiles*, UNDP World Bank Water and Sanitation Program, Washington DC.

Solo, T. M. (1998), *Competition in water and sanitation; the role of small-scale entrepreneurs*, Note 165, The World Bank, Washington D.C.

WHO and UNICEF (2000), *Global Water Supply and Sanitation Assessment 2000 Report*, World Health Organization and United Nations Children's Fund, Geneva and New York.

World Bank (2003), *Dar es Salaam Water Supply and Sanitation Project: Project Appraisal Document* 25249 - TA, World Bank, Washington DC.